Earth's RAINIEST PLACES

BY BAILEY O'CONNELL

Gareth Stevens
PUBLISHING

Please visit our website, www.garethstevens.com. For a free color catalog of all our high-quality books, call toll free 1-800-542-2595 or fax 1-877-542-2596.

Library of Congress Cataloging-in-Publication Data

O'Connell, Bailey.
Earth's rainiest places / by Bailey O'Connell.
p. cm. — (Earth's most extreme places)
Includes index.
ISBN 978-1-4824-1910-8 (pbk.)
ISBN 978-1-4824-1909-2 (6-pack)
ISBN 978-1-4824-1912-2 (library binding)
1. Rain and rainfall — Juvenile literature. 2. Weather — Juvenile literature. I. O'Connell, Bailey, author. II. Title.
QC924.7 O26 2015
551.577—d23

First Edition

Published in 2015 by
Gareth Stevens Publishing
111 East 14th Street, Suite 349
New York, NY 10003

Copyright © 2015 Gareth Stevens Publishing

Designer: Katelyn E. Reynolds
Editor: Therese Shea

Photo credits: Cover, p. 1 Liysa/Perspectives/Getty Images; cover, pp. 1–24 (background texture) ArtTDi/Shutterstock.com; p. 5 FamVeld/Shutterstock.com; p. 7 (map) MattWright/Wikipedia.com; p. 7 (main) Michael Utech/E+/Getty Images; p. 9 (map) Filip Bjorkman/Shutterstock.com; p. 9 (main) John Henry Claude Wilson/Robert Harding World Imagery/Getty Images; p. 11 (map) Saravask, based on work by Planemad and Nichalp/Wikipedia.com; p. 11 (main) T photography/Shutterstock.com; p. 13 (map) Stannered/Wikipedia.com; p. 13 (main) Luis Robayo/AFP/Getty Images; p. 15 Merkushev Vasiliy/Shutterstock.com; p. 17 Dennis K. Johnson/Lonely Planet Images/Getty Images; p. 18 Sharon Eisenzopf/Shutterstock.com; p. 19 (map) Theshibboleth/Wikipedia.com; p. 19 (main) Laszlo Podor Photography/Moment/Getty Images; p. 21 Jim McKinley/Moment Open/Getty Images.

Printed in the United States of America

CPSIA compliance information: Batch #CW15GS: For further information contact Gareth Stevens, New York, New York at 1-800-542-2595.

CONTENTS

Words in the glossary appear in **bold** type the first time they are used in the text.

RAIN, RAIN, GO AWAY!

Have you ever had to stay inside all day because it was raining? Sometimes, it may rain several days in a row. However, at some point, the sun comes out, so you can get outside to play again.

There are some places on Earth where the rain doesn't stop for a long, long time. Would you want to live there? You'd have to live your life very differently. Read on to find out how people survive in the rainiest places on Earth!

The rain can stop our plans, but it's needed to keep plants and animals healthy.
Too much rain can have a harmful effect on our world, however.

MOUNT WAIALEALE

Mount Waialeale (wy-ah-lay-AH-lay) on the Hawaiian island of Kauai was once thought to be the rainiest place on Earth. It rains about 350 days a year there, adding up to about 450 inches (1,140 cm). That means its green slopes are much like a **swamp**.

The mountain rises 5,148 feet (1,569 m) above sea level and is often covered with clouds. Mount Waialeale's rainfall feeds Hawaii's only rivers as well as several waterfalls. In fact, the powerful water traveling down the mountain has carved **canyons** into Mount Waialeale's sides.

THAT'S EXTREME!

In 1982, Mount Waialeale received 683 inches (1,735 cm) of rain—or nearly 57 feet (17.4 m)!

Mount Waialeale

Only a few miles from Mount Waialeale, the amount of rain drops to only 10 inches (25 cm) a year!

HAWAII

RECORD BREAKERS IN INDIA

Cherrapunji (chehr-uh-PUHN-jee), a village in northeastern India, calls itself the "wettest place on Earth." It **averages** 464 inches (1,179 cm) of rain a year. That's almost 39 feet (12 m)! However, another, smaller village about 10 miles (16 km) away may be rainier. Mawsynram (maw-SEEN-rahm) averages 467 inches (1,186 cm) of rain per year.

Almost 90 percent of northeastern India's rain falls between May and October. During this time, a weather event called a monsoon takes place.

THAT'S EXTREME!

Cherrapunji holds the record for the greatest rainfall in a year. Between August 1860 and July 1861, it rained 1,042 inches (2,647 cm)!

About 10,000 people live in Cherrapunji.

INDIA

Mawsynram

Cherrapunji

MONSOON!

A monsoon is a wind pattern that brings heavy rains. Monsoons are caused by temperature differences in the air over land and sea. In summer, hot air over land rises. Cool air over water then rushes in to take its place. This air is full of **moisture** from the sea. It warms, rises into the air to form clouds, and then falls as rain.

The winds that bring rain to Cherrapunji and Mawsynram are called the southwest monsoon. It blows off the Bay of Bengal.

THAT'S EXTREME!

During winter, the monsoon winds change direction. Most summer monsoons come from the west, and most winter monsoons come from the east.

Farmers in India need the monsoon to bring rain each year to grow crops. However, too much rain can harm their farms.

southwest monsoon

INDIA

Bay of Bengal

PUERTO LOPEZ

Recently, a town in South America has been crowned the rainiest place on Earth. Puerto Lopez is found near the western coast of Colombia. Between April 1960 and February 2012, it received an average rainfall of more than 507 inches (1,288 cm) a year! That's more than Mawsynram in India.

Puerto Lopez's location between the Pacific Ocean and a mountain range is the reason for its amazing amount of rainfall. The mountains to its east stop rain clouds from traveling further inland.

THAT'S EXTREME!

In 1984 and 1985, it rained every single day in Puerto Lopez!

Puerto
Lopez

COLOMBIA

SOUTH
AMERICA

Incredibly, Puerto Lopez had 937 inches
(2,380 cm) of rain in 1984!

WHERE DOES THE RAIN GO?

Since some of these rainy places receive many, many feet of rain each year, you might wonder what happens to all that water. It either **seeps** into the ground or becomes runoff. Runoff is the water that flows over the land and into rivers, lakes, and oceans. There, the rain **evaporates** to become clouds, and the cycle continues.

However, in some places, the rain can't seep into the ground or can't seep fast enough. It might not be able to flow into rivers and lakes either. That's when floods occur.

RAIN'S EFFECTS

In many parts of India, monsoons are welcomed to break the hot, dry weather and provide water for farms and everyday life. In the dry season in parts of India, people must walk miles for water. But monsoon flooding can sweep away an entire community, so the rains are feared as well.

Around the world, people fear flooding due to extreme rainfall. Even a small amount of floodwater can knock people off their feet, ruin houses and cars, and make water unsafe for drinking and bathing.

THAT'S EXTREME!

Almost a billion people in India depend on the monsoon rains for crops that become their food.

Flooding may occur in cities where the ground is covered by matter that can't absorb, or take in, water.

118

17

RAINIEST IN THE UNITED STATES?

There are some very rainy cities in the United States, too. In the South, Mobile, Alabama, gets a bit more than 65 inches (165 cm) of rain a year. In the Northwest, Astoria, Oregon, receives 67 inches (170 cm) of rain each year, while Forks, Washington, gets close to 99 inches (251 cm).

However, the location of the wettest US city may surprise you. Hilo, Hawaii, averages more than 127 inches (323 cm) of rain a year, thanks to the moist air of the Pacific Ocean.

Astoria, Oregon

Many people travel to Hawaii because of its warm weather.
Hilo's rainfall means beautiful rainforests and waterfalls await visitors.

Forks, Washington
Astoria, Oregon

UNITED STATES

Mobile, Alabama

Hilo, Hawaii

19

CLIMATE CHANGE

Many scientists think that **climate change** is causing more rainfall. As temperatures around the world increase, more water evaporates and then falls as rain. Some places aren't prepared for major rainstorms and floods. People there have to start building better roads, bridges, and **sewer systems**. They have to move away from oceans and rivers, too.

However, cutting down on the amount of harmful gases **released** into the air because of human activities may help slow climate change. Our Earth-friendly actions may help us stay dry in the future!

HOW RAINY? AVERAGE RAINFALL PER YEAR

—— Puerto Lopez, Colombia: 507 inches (1,288 cm)

—— Mawsynram, India: 467 inches (1,186 cm)

—— Cherrapunji, India: 464 inches (1,179 cm)

—— Mount Waialeale, Hawaii: 450 inches (1,168 cm)

—— Hilo, Hawaii: 127 inches (323 cm)

—— Mobile, Alabama: 65 inches (165 cm)

Mobile, Alabama

21

GLOSSARY

average: to add numbers together and divide the sum by the number of numbers

canyon: a deep valley with steep sides

climate change: long-term change in Earth's climate, caused partly by human activities such as burning oil and natural gas

evaporate: to change from a liquid to a gas

moisture: water in the air

release: to let go

seep: to pass or escape through small openings very slowly and in small quantities

sewer system: a man-made, usually underground passageway to carry off waste and surface water

swamp: an area with trees that is covered with water at least part of the time

FOR MORE INFORMATION

BOOKS

Kalman, Bobbie, and Rebecca Sjonger. *The Water Cycle*. New York, NY: Crabtree Publishing Company, 2006.

Koponen, Libby. *Floods*. New York, NY: Children's Press, 2009.

Simon, Seymour. *Seymour Simon's Extreme Earth Records*. San Francisco, CA: Chronicle Books, 2012.

WEBSITES

The Rainiest Places in the World: Exploring Global Precipitation
www.decodedscience.com/rainiest-places-in-the-world/26982
Read more about rain, monsoons, and other weather events.

The Water Cycle
www.kidzone.ws/water/
This is a fun guide to the water cycle.

Where, Exactly, Is the Wettest Place on Earth?
www.weather.com/news/science/nature/wettest-place-earth-20130529
Learn more about the hunt for the rainiest place on Earth.

INDEX